From Ashes to Beauty

RECOVERING FROM TRAUMA THROUGH THE SPIRIT

LILA COOK

Copyright © 2022 by Lila Cook

All rights reserved.

No part of this book may be reproduced in any form or by any electronic or mechanical means, including information storage and retrieval systems, without written permission from the author, except for the use of brief quotations in a book review.

Photo credit for front cover: Neenah Cook

Scriptures marked AMP are taken from the AMPLIFIED BIBLE (AMP): Scripture taken from the AMPLIFIED® BIBLE, Copyright © 1954, 1958, 1962, 1964, 1965, 1987 by the Lockman Foundation Used by Permission.

Scriptures marked NLT are taken from the HOLY BIBLE, NEW LIVING TRANSLATION (NLT): Scriptures taken from the HOLY BIBLE, NEW LIVING TRANSLATION, Copyright© 1996, 2004, 2007 by Tyndale House Foundation. Used by permission of Tyndale House Publishers, Inc., Carol Stream, Illinois 60188. All rights reserved. Used by permission.

Scriptures marked KJV are taken from the KING JAMES VERSION (KJV): KING JAMES VERSION, public domain.

Scriptures marked NIV are taken from the NEW INTERNATIONAL VERSION (NIV): Scripture taken from THE HOLY BIBLE, NEW INTERNATIONAL VERSION ®. Copyright© 1973, 1978, 1984, 2011 by Biblica, Inc.TM. Used by permission of Zondervan

Scriptures marked NKJV are taken from the NEW KING JAMES VERSION (NKJV): Scripture taken from the NEW KING JAMES VERSION®. Copyright© 1982 by Thomas Nelson, Inc. Used by permission. All rights reserved.

Scriptures marked ESV are taken from the THE HOLY BIBLE, ENGLISH STANDARD VERSION (ESV): Scriptures taken from THE HOLY BIBLE, ENGLISH STANDARD VERSION ® Copyright© 2001 by Crossway, a publishing ministry of Good News Publishers. Used by permission.

Scripture quotations marked (NASB) are taken from the NEW AMERICAN STANDARD BIBLE®, Copyright© 1960, 1962, 1963, 1968, 1971, 1972, 1973, 1975, 1977, 1995 by The Lockman Foundation. Used by permission.

Introduction

Many people have suffered from trauma and abuse. Because of this, the cycle of abuse and trauma is handed down from one generation to the next, before healing occurs. If this sounds like you, you're not alone! It is my hope and prayer that this devotional assists you in the healing process. You deserve to be whole. One of the reasons Jesus came was to restore all that was lost. If your experience has left you feeling lost in life, then this devotional is for you!

I decided to be open with you about some of my abusive and traumatic experiences in hopes that you will find your own voice from your experiences in this area as well. The more honest you are with yourself and with God, the more you will see recovery in your life.

As a very small child and through my teen years I was abused. Most of the abuse came through my mom, as my dad was largely neglectful & unapproachable to me. To be honest, I was terrified of both of my parents & found myself craving unconditional love, warmth & approval.

    As a child, I was slapped with bare hands across my face, and beaten with belts and switches or anything that was within reach.

INTRODUCTION

One of the most difficult things for me to understand is why I was being beaten. I was told at times that I was sassing. However, I was a very quiet child, I spent the majority of my childhood as the family wallflower because I learned my lessons by observing my parents punish my siblings. I was timid and mostly silent. I can't imagine myself sassing my parents at all. I already knew better.

When I was nine years old, my parents divorced. My mom began going to bars and brought men home afterward. One particular night, I had waited through the night for my mom to come home. I was worried sick that something had happened to her. Finally, in the early morning hours, my mom came home with a man I didn't know. They were walking into her bedroom. The man asked, "what about her"? Pointing to me. My mom said, "she doesn't matter".

I had stayed up all night waiting for her. I had the house spotless, and dinner made, and I couldn't comprehend why I didn't matter to my mom. These words stayed in my mind for most of my life.

There were other incidents that hurt me deeply, much, more than I can mention here within these pages.

As a young child, my mom mocked me in front of family and friends at gatherings. One example is that my mom would laugh and make fun of my "knot knees and pigeon toes". Calling my name from across the yard, she said, "Lila come here". She was calling me to join the adults. She forced me to walk toward her while she and my aunts and uncles laughed and poked fun at my knotted knees and pigeon toes. I was so crushed! I felt imperfect, unlovable, self-conscious, and unworthy.

As an adolescent, I was forced to go to the bars with my mom, because she didn't want to worry about me being home alone. Looking back, I was around 12 -13 years old; plenty old enough to stay home by myself. That made me wonder if she had another purpose for taking me to the bars.

INTRODUCTION

While at the bars, many men approached me and made sexual advances. I just sat there stiffly, fearful to move and draw attention to myself. I ignored the men who approached me. Some would try to bribe me so they could have sexual favors. These nights usually ended with my mom in the bathroom throwing up in the toilet due to drinking too much. I was always right by her side, mopping her forehead with a cold paper towel and quietly telling her that she would be alright. These weekends continued for approximately two years of my life.

As I grew older and was able to stay home, my mom would bring men home. She went through several relationships with men. Many of these relationships were unhealthy and dangerous, not only for my mom but for me as well.

One man had spent time in prison. On one particular night, while he was at our house, he drew a knife on my mom and cut the phone lines. While he waved the knife around, threatening to kill my mom, I snuck up the stairs and used the phone in my mom's bedroom to call the police. They arrived and took the man away. I don't like to think about what might have happened that night.

Yet another man came to our house (my brother was there with me) with a loaded gun. The man only had one leg and used crutches. He waved the gun at my brother and me, drunken out of his mind, demanding to know where our mom was. My brother and I moved together simultaneously. We grabbed his crutches, and my brother took the gun away from him. The man fell to the floor and the gun went off, the shots hitting the floor. We then gave the man's crutches back and pushed him out the door.

On another occasion, my mom had a man over and she was sending him to the store for alcohol and snack items. She requested that I go with this man to assure that we got the right items. We never left our driveway! Once I was in the car, the man began to touch me inappropriately. I was frightened and frozen. He offered me four hundred dollars to give him sexual favors. I said nothing, I was terrified and thinking of a way to escape the car as I had been locked in. While the man continued molesting me, I found the lock to the car door in the darkness of the night. I jumped from the car, my heart pounding in my ears. As I raced up to the house, I saw that my mom was watching from the window. How long had she been there? Why hadn't she come to my rescue? In fact, why had she sent me off with a stranger? These questions haunted me for years.

The trail of men was endless, and my mom was married several times. The son of one husband also molested me. I literally lived in a fight or flight mode...a war zone where I continuously had to protect myself. I felt insecure, unsafe, lonely, and guarded. It was during these years that deep depression and anxiety set in for me.

The beatings continued until I was 17 years old. One night while my mom was out, a couple of school friends stopped over at our house. I didn't have many friends; I was busy hiding behind my shame. We did innocent things. We played games, talked, and watched television. Suddenly, my mom returned home for something, and I immediately knew I was in trouble for having friends over. My mom took her foot and literally shoved each of my friends out the front door. I was so embarrassed.

The next morning when my mom woke up, she began to question me about what I had done with my friends. I was honest with her and told her what we had done, but she didn't believe me. When I look back on her actions, It seemed she was projecting the things she had experienced onto me. She yelled at me loudly in her anger. She said that I was to never have friends over while she was away. She then got out a leather belt and began to beat me wildly all over my body. I was so burned out from the beatings...I just sat there and took it. I believe I had reached the end of my emotions and my spirit was broken. It hurt badly, but I felt mentally numb. I didn't fight it. Because I wasn't crying, or trying to avoid the belt, my mom grew all the angrier because I didn't respond. The angrier she got, the more she whipped me with the belt, until she was breathless and could beat me no longer. That was the last time I was

INTRODUCTION

physically beaten. I packed my bag and left that day. I went to stay with my best friend who understood my situation. My friend's mom spoke to my mom on the phone. I don't know what was said even to this day. I didn't want to know what my mom said, because I feared the pain it would cause me. I never returned home to live. I was soon to be eighteen years old, I got a job, and stayed with my friend.

Eventually, I married the love of my life, my high-school sweetheart. We are still together 43 years later! My husband went through my healing process with me during our marriage. It was not an easy process, as I often projected my feelings onto my husband. I had a lot of healing to do and only God could help me to heal, and HE DID! Today, we celebrate our life together and are thankful to Abba for the work he has done in our lives.

I did have a relationship with my mom before I got married. However, the relationship was strained. I was always under scrutiny and unnecessary judgment from her. Though there were many more tragic events to take place during my adulthood concerning my mom, as we drew near the end of her life, she grew very ill with cardiopulmonary disease. My sister and I cared for my mom, so she could stay in her home. Her very last words to me were, "you are a rebel, you always have been, and you always will be". She laughed as if that were very funny.

Initially, those words stung because I had always thought of myself as obedient to my mom. Then, as I was praying one day, I embraced the term "rebel", as in heretic; a person who doesn't follow social norms. I have never been a follower socially, as I normally carved my own path. As quiet and shy as I was. I felt very alone in life and have found comfort In God. Even as a small child, I would go to my room to talk to Jesus. Those moments remain precious to me to this day.

When my mom passed into eternity, I was very melancholy because we didn't have the relationship that I so desired with her. Despite the abuse, I still love my mom very much! I came to understand that my mom acted out of her own brokenness. That made me feel very sad. But, I rejoice now in her going home. I know she's with our loving Father and she is now whole. Someday, I will join her and for the first time ever, we will embrace freely, and without tension between us, as I know she is no longer broken, and neither am I!

My relationship with my dad was distant. He really didn't want much to do with me or my siblings. When we finally got together as adults, it was awkward because his spouse didn't care for the relationship I was attempting to build with my dad. After my dad's wife passed away, my dad immediately called me. Eventually, In his older years, he wanted to be with his family. I believe he was living in the past as if we were still children. He requested to move to where I lived. I found him a home in Michigan, in our city, and one of my brothers drove him from Arizona. Eventually, he became ill and was unable to stay in his own home independently. Because I was attending college and worked full time, we had to find an assisted living facility for him. This is where my dad stayed until his death. God had restored my relationship with my dad. Before he became ill, we went shopping together, I read scriptures from the Bible to him, prayed with him and we went for long walks.

I'm glad I had those last years with my dad! We finally developed a relationship together!

It's essential for you to know that I am in perfect peace today regarding my upbringing. I understand that I lost much of a "normal" childhood and even adolescence and young adulthood. Though there was not much joy in my past, I am healed from all my brokenness! I am no longer crushed in spirit. I am joyful today because God has provided a way for me to help others who have experienced similar backgrounds.

If at any time you feel overwhelmed with your healing process, you should seek out professional advice.

My hope is that you regain your joy and find happiness and peace in your life through God's love for you and through Jesus's finished work on the cross despite any trauma you have experienced in your life. You have resurrection power living within you! This power is from the same Spirit that raised Christ from the dead. All things are possible with God my friends. May your freedom from bondage begin within the brokenness you may be feeling.

I have prayed for you, that you will become aware that Jesus lives within you and that you will accept your healing from God. You are loved beyond measure exactly where you are right now!

Let us begin the healing process...

Preface

I have prayed for you, my friends; my hope is that you are freed from the bondage that you have endured in your lifetime, through what I believe is a spirit-filled devotional and memoir.

This devotional was written with you in mind! The main focus of the devotional is your recovery from trauma and abuse through the truth of the gospel and the finished work of the cross of Jesus. The most important message you should take from these pages is that you are loved beyond measure by our Father, and by Jesus exactly where you are at this very moment!

You may have been told that there is something you need to do to earn God's love. But there is nothing special you need to do to obtain God's love. Jesus already provided you with all you need. You are Abba's temple right now! The only thing lacking is your understanding of this great love God has for you.

I pray that this devotional changes your mind about the beliefs you have been taught in the past and that you realize that Abba Father is not vengeful or punishing towards you. For there is now, therefore, no condemnation for those in Christ Jesus and you are in Christ Jesus.

May freedom come to you through the truth of the gospel of Jesus Christ, your Living Hope! May your broken heart be mended as Jesus binds up your wounds. Trauma, guilt, fear, shame, and torment will be far behind you, as you learn the truth of Father's love concerning you! I pray that you become aware that through the resurrection and the finished work of the cross, you are whole, complete, and filled with the fullness of God! God created you and said you were good, he loves all he made, including you!

In the blessings of our Lord,
    Lila Cook

Knowing God's True Nature

God is love. Whoever lives in love lives in God, and God in him.
John 4:16 (NIV)

Knowing God and understanding his nature is key to enjoying a face-to-face relationship with him. Many people know *about* God, but not everyone understands his true character. Scripture makes the point that God IS love. The terms "Love and God" are used interchangeably. Because you have love within you, you live in God, and he lives in you! The fact that God is within you is Love's/God's response to his creation. Abba adores what he has created, and he longs for a relationship with you. Love never fails.

Memoir

Though I was introduced to the church at the age of four years old, I Still, did not grasp the concept that God loved me without conditions. I struggled through mid- adulthood without understanding Father's true nature. I viewed God as my judge and someone I had to please to make it to eternity. I was continually searching for Abba's approval, desperate to know him personally. During my adult years, I began to look to Father for a revelation of his love and grace. His love overwhelmed me because love never fails!

Prayer

Father, I bring your beautiful creation before you and I pray over them, that their eyes be opened to your generous mercy and your unconditional love for them.

Song/YouTube: God Really Loves Us: Crowder & Dante Bowe

Chosen Before Time Began

For he chose us in him before the creation of the world to be holy and blameless in his sight Ephesians 1:4 (NIV)

He has saved us and called us to a holy life - not because of anything we've done, but because of his own purpose and grace. This grace was given us in Christ Jesus before the beginning of time
2 Timothy 1:9 (NIV)

Imagine! You were chosen in Christ BEFORE you were born and even BEFORE the foundations of the earth. You cannot work your way or earn your way into God's grace. Rather, it is a free gift to you, and it is manifested through the finished work of the cross in Christ.

Memoir
When I learned that we had all been in God's plans from the begin-

ning of time, I felt self-worth and God's approval for the first time in my life. My life, up to that point, had no purpose except for the pain I had endured. Knowing that God thought of me before the beginning of time brought the security that I had always longed for throughout my entire life!

Prayer

Abba, thank you for extending your grace and favor unto me. Not because of anything I can do or I have done, but through what Jesus has done. I'm grateful that you chose me before the beginning of time! God called me to live a holy and blameless life. I realize that I can't live this life holy and blameless on my own. This lifestyle can only be accomplished IN Christ Jesus and through his grace. Scripture points out that this is Abba's choosing. This has nothing to do with my works, as you have chosen me before the foundations of this world, and by your grace, I will live a holy life.

Song/YouTube: The One You Love: Chandler Moore

Alive In Christ – Dead To Sin

His appointment with death was once off (once and for all). As far as sin is concerned, he is dead. The reason for his death was to take away the sin of the world; his LIFE NOW exhibits OUR union with the life of God. [11] This reasoning is equally relevant to you. Calculate the cross; there can only be one logical conclusion: he died your death: that means you died to sin and are NOW ALIVE to God. Sin-consciousness can never again feature in your future! You are in Christ; his lordship is the authority of this union.
Romans 6: 10-11 (Mirror Bible)

You may be experiencing feelings of being unworthy and you may be sin-conscious and you may believe your nature is under the law of sin and death. Now that you have awakened, you know that you died in Christ, and have been resurrected with him, sin has no dominion over you. God's grace and love do not give us a license to sin, as some believe. Just the opposite is true. The indwelling of Christ living in you causes you to lose the desire to sin or to be sin-conscious. Your entire focus will be on the grace and love God has for you. You are in him, and he is in you! He is yours, and you are his!

Memoir

For most of my life, I felt I was unworthy of my salvation! In fact, I was unsure of my salvation. I also carried a great deal of shame in my heart because of the continuous condemnation I was under from my environment growing up and because of religious teachings of being sin conscious. What I learned later in my life was that Jesus took care of sin once and for all on the cross! When he died, our sinful nature died with him; when he rose, we also rose with him as a new creation! No more condemnation.

Prayer

Father, thank you that your son's work on the cross was sufficient to destroy the power of sin and death (the law). Help me to realize that this is in nothing I can do or have done; rather, the destruction of sin (the law) was finished in the work of Jesus on the cross. Show me your unconditional love and grace over me through your Spirit. Make me aware of my rightful position in you through the final sacrifice of Jesus.

Song/YouTube: Resurrection Power: Chris Tomlin

The Peace of God Over Anxiety & Fear

Do not be anxious about anything, but in everything by prayer and supplication with thanksgiving, let your request be known to God. ⁷ And the peace of God, which surpasses all understanding, will guard your hearts and minds in Christ Jesus.
Philippians 4: 6-7 (NKJV)

Most often, anxiety is rooted in fear. Fear of not knowing an outcome, fear of what the future holds, fear of how you will survive, fear for your health, and fear of death. Basically, fear of the unknown. Fear and anxiety are not of God because fear has torment, and we have already established that God is love. The perfect love of God sends fear running! If you will closely examine your fears and anxieties, you will discover that much of what you fear and are anxious over comes from your own human thoughts and never comes to pass! That is why we must take our worries to Jesus through the Spirit and bypass our human thoughts. We must put on the mind of Christ!

. . .

Memoir

I spent the majority of my life, especially my younger years, filled with anxiety and fear. I believe much of the anxiety was a result of living in an abusive home. I spent my energy attempting to avoid family conflict and not knowing what traumatic event would occur next. This was so incredibly draining and unhealthy because most of my time was spent in a fight or flight mode. It resulted in years of being physically ill and fatigued. Once I learned I could put matters into God's care, the anxiety and fear lifted. I learned to trust again because I finally understood that Abba was reliable and dependable and that I could trust him with my deepest concerns! I learned to have the mind of Christ!

Prayer

Jesus, I bring everything to you in prayer. I know you are approachable, and I know you love me and care for me. I also know that you care about all that concerns me. I'm not imposing upon you when I take everything that worries me to you in prayer. Thank you for giving me your peace, which is beyond my understanding. Help me to think of what you think and say about me,

Song/YouTube: Fear Is Not My Future: Brandon Lake & Chandler Moore

A Sound Mind

God has not given us a spirit of fear but of power, love, and a SOUND MIND.
11 Timothy 1:7 (KJV)

We have discussed anxiety caused by fear and the fact that God gives us peace beyond understanding. Let's delve a little deeper! 11 Timothy 1:7 tells us that God has given us a spirit of love, power, and a sound mind, but *not* a spirit of fear.

There may be times in life when you feel overwhelmed by your circumstances. Feelings of being overwhelmed can make you feel that you are not grounded emotionally or mentally or as if things are falling to pieces. However, you absolutely must take God at his word. When things seem out of control, remember that these situations are under God's control! In the reality of life, multiple circumstances are not within your control. In fact, the majority of situations you worry about never come to pass. Why should you spend your time in fear, worry, and feeling as if you are in need of a mental adjustment when God has promised you a sound mind, love, and power?

Memoir

Before I knew of God's love for me, I feared many things; I feared death, an eternity in hell, demons, and my future. I feared everything in life. Once, Abba showed me his love for me, and I understood that perfect love drives out fear. I found overwhelming peace in my heart and spirit for the first time in my life. Thank you, Abba, for giving me a spirit of love, power, and a sound mind! I understand that even when I feel overwhelmed by circumstances, you are in control of every outcome in my life. Since you are in control, I will let go of worry, fear, and feelings that I do not have a clear and sound mind!

Prayer

I thank you, Abba, for giving me a sound mind: a mind of power and love directly from you! I don't need to rely on my emotions or my mentality to gain peace. My peace comes from you alone. I saturate myself in your love, and I realize the power and strength you've gifted to me in my life! I have a sound mind!

Song/YouTube: Sound Mind: Melissa Helser

God's Grace Is Sufficient

But he said to me, "my grace is sufficient for you; my power is made perfect in weakness". Therefore, I will boast all the more gladly about my weaknesses, so that Christ's power may rest on me.
11 Corinthians 12:9 (NIV)

God's power is made perfect in your weaknesses! This scripture isn't saying that God's power is sufficient in your strengths, but rather in our weaknesses. God intervenes even when you make mistakes in life and even when you make a mess of things. God's grace always comes to your rescue, especially in your weaknesses. Grace has no beginning and no end. Grace isn't applied when you behave well but is sufficient in areas where you are weak.

Memoir

Recently, I had been fussing over a mistake I had repeated from the past. I spent two days kicking myself around until guilt and shame settled into my thoughts and consumed my energy as they occupied my mind. The next morning, when I woke up, I had to make a decision ...I had to decide if I was going to continue to wallow in the guilt and shame I was feeling. God must have worked a miracle over me during the night because as I was waking, I heard a voice within me saying, "this is the perfect situation for my strength, and you will experience the fullness of my grace in your weakness".

Suddenly, peace beyond my understanding encompassed my being, and I knew that I would be alright, despite making my own mistake again.

Prayer
Lord, show me the fullness of your grace in my weaknesses! Help me to understand that when I am weak, you are strong on my behalf. Father, let me see that grace is Jesus, the restorer of all things. Let me hear your voice telling me that there is not one situation in my circumstances that makes your grace non-effective.

Song/YouTube: Sufficient for Today : Maryanne J. George

But the Advocate, the Holy Spirit, whom the Father will send in my name, will teach you all things and will remind you of everything I have said to you.
John 14:26 (NIV)

When the Spirit of truth comes, he will guide you into ALL truth, for he will not speak on his own authority, but whatever he hears he will speak, and he will declare the things that are to come.
John 16:13 (ESV)

These scriptures are prophetic. They concern Jesus sending the Holy Spirit to lead you into all truth, to teach you, to guide you, and to comfort you, in addition to helping you in life's journey. Since Jesus returned to the Father, after finishing his work on the cross, he has already given the Holy Spirit to you, which he promised! The Holy Spirit is often referred to as your helper and your comforter. At any given time in your life, you can ask Holy Spirit to lead you into truth, whether it be a decision you need to make, questions you may have, fear you may be facing, if you are in need of wisdom or knowledge, in times of confusion or even if you are experiencing doubt, you can be assured that the Holy Spirit will bring you into ALL truth! He will comfort you and help you, and lead in the direction you should go.

Memoir

Years ago, while in college, I had a professor who said, "if in doubt, leave it out"! Of course, he was speaking about writing English essays! But I got a hold of that wisdom and was able to apply it to multiple situations in my life. From that point forward, I used that knowledge in many situations in my life. I learned that if I feel doubt or confusion, I make no decisions, and I do not move until I hear from the Spirit of Truth. I follow the peace the Holy Spirit places in my heart and in my spirit. If we follow the Spirit of ALL truth in our lives, it will save us much heartache!

Prayer

I pray for every reader of this devotional, Father, to bring all truth to my readers so that they will experience the leading of the Holy Spirit. I speak deliverance from confusion, fear, doubt, and unrest in your spirit. Lead them into all truth through the manifestation of knowledge, wisdom, peace, and understanding by the Holy Spirit. Bring comfort to those who have broken hearts. Amen!

Song/YouTube: Spirit Lead Me/Spirit Break Out: Michael Ketterer & Kim Walker Smith

Leaning On Jesus

Come unto me, all who labor and are heavy laden, and I will give you rest.
Matthew 11:28 (NIV)

Have you been weary, heavy burdened, burned out on religion? LOOK UP SCRIPTURE
Jeremiah 29:11 (NIV)

In other words, are you tired, depressed, anxious, or weary of religion (the law)? You don't need to carry those burdens any longer. They were not meant for you to carry in the first place. In fact, you were not meant to carry any of the cares you have taken upon yourself! If you hold onto life's burdens, then fatigue, depression, and anxiety will set in. This is how you become weary and heavy-laden. But you are not on this journey alone...you have Christ living within you. You are his dwelling place! You are IN Christ, and he is IN you. You are one with him because of the resurrection. Any cares that might arise are meant to be the responsibility of Jesus! You need to give your cares to Jesus as they arise in your mind in order to stop your thought process from internalizing them. This means you must LET GO of what troubles you by putting your trust in Jesus because you know he loves you, and he takes care of those he loves. God has good plans to prosper you and not cause you any harm. His plans are to give you hope and a future. Jesus's yoke is easy, and his burdens are light. He delights in you coming to him with what troubles you,

Memoir

There was a time in my life when I was not aware of the length Jesus would go to carry my problems. In looking back, I see him taking my burdens as a part of the finished work of the cross. Through my healing process, I learned to recognize when I was taking issues upon myself. I began to realize this sooner rather than later and before anxiety, weariness and depression had a chance to settle into my heart and mind, Now, as soon as my thought process within my mind begins to take shape, I speak out loud, "Jesus, I let go of this concern and cast all my burdens onto you because I know you love me and I can trust you to take care of it".

Prayer

Jesus, I'm so thankful that I can take what troubles me to you! I realize that you will resolve my issues and that you do not want me to carry them. I'm incapable of carrying these burdens myself because they make me depressed, anxious, weary, tired, and burned out. I know the plans you have for me are good, and you will prosper me and cause me no harm. I cast every weight that hinders me upon you!

Song/YouTube: Leaning: Matt Maher & Lizzie Morgan

Not Lost

What do you think? If a man has a hundred sheep, and one of them gets lost, will he not leave the ninety-nine on the mountain and go in search of the one that is lost?
Matthew 18:12 (AMP)

This is a parable taught by Jesus. Jesus is saying that he would go to any length to find a person who was lost. If you're feeling lost, have no fear because Jesus has found you! Perhaps you are not yet aware that Jesus has found you? But trust me, he knows exactly where you are and how you feel and will meet you right where you are in your journey. You are not an afterthought to God. Remember, you are loved beyond measure! Abba took time to create you, his hands shaped your form, and he breathed his life into you, making you a living soul! Though you may believe you've blown it or messed things up badly, Jesus is the very first one to search for you, his beloved creation. Please, don't allow your five senses to dictate how God feels about you. You must believe what he says about you, not what your thoughts and feelings say. You may feel that you've gotten off the path of God. But Jesus has never once lost you! Abba is continuously and relentlessly in pursuit of you. Simply turn to him (within yourself, his dwelling place) and become aware that He would go to any length to find you!

Memoir

I previously believed that I could be lost eternally if I got on the wrong path or if I sinned in some way. I believed that my Father would torture me forever in hell. I lived in fear that I could lose my salvation and it caused cognitive dissonance (believing two ways or being double minded in a belief). I learned differently, I changed my mind, which means to repent. I now know that Jesus keeps me carefully under his watch and that none shall perish but have everlasting life! I have put on the mind of Christ because it is no longer I who live, but Christ who lives in me. What a relief to understand that Abba has a plan for my life. How precious it is to know that Jesus pursues me endlessly. His love for me gives me reassurance that I can never be lost or separated from his love and care!

Prayer

Jesus thank you for your loving kindness towards me. Bring to light the truth that I will never be lost or separated from your love. This is your choice for me, Jesus. You promised me that you would never leave or forsake me and that I'm never left alone. I'm grateful that you are in pursuit of me out of your great love for me. Thank you for making me your dwelling place.

Song/YouTube: Never Lost: Joe L Barnes, Lizzie Morgan & Melvin Crispell

A Mistaken Identity

SIN CONSCIOUSNESS

There is therefore now no condemnation to those who are in Christ Jesus, who do not walk according to the flesh, but according to the Spirit, for the law of the Spirit of life in Christ Jesus has made me free from the law of sin and death.
Romans 8: 1-2 (NKJV)

John the Baptist sees Jesus and exclaimed, "Behold the Lamb of God Who Takes away the sin of the world".
John 1:29 (NIV)

Don't be confused! Those you see as evil are functioning from a mistaken identity, that is, they have not yet awakened to the fact that they are blameless before God due to the finished work of the cross. The people who cause offense in your life do not yet grasp that Christ lives within them and that Jesus took away the sin of the world. They are still operating from the law of sin and death. Because of this they frequently harm others, acting out of a sin-consciousness, rather than the love of God. It is often said that "hurt people, hurt people". Those who are causing pain to you are hurting for lack of knowledge that Jesus came to take away the sin of the entire world. Those who cause pain do not yet recognize that Jesus' sacrifice was for the world including themselves. Knowing this should help you to understand that the people in your life causing you pain have not yet had a revelation of Christ within themselves.

Memoir

Since I was raised in an abusive home and lived in continuous traumatic circumstances, I was damaged and broken spiritually, mentally, physically, and emotionally by those who claimed to love me. I was in a continuous state of confusion. I didn't understand that my parents were broken also, Remember, hurt people hurt people! Later in my life, Abba taught me that those who had caused me damage were still functioning under the law (a mistaken identity) and did not understand their right position in Christ. Today, I hold no offense against those who caused me harm. Jesus has healed my wounds and I am free from the damage that was done. I now grasp the fact that they had a mistaken identity, not realizing who they were in Christ, just as I once did.

Prayer

Abba Daddy, help us to understand that broken people hurt others through mistaken identity, as they do not grasp that Jesus came to save the world from the law of sin and death through the finished work of the cross. As I forgive those who have injured me, set me free from offense. Thank you for your healing me and binding up of my wounds so that I can love and understand the brokenness in others. Open my eyes to the relentless love of Christ!

Song/YouTube: Gone: Elevation Music

Forgiveness

For I will be merciful toward their iniquities, and I will remember their sins no more
Hebrews 8:12

God promised he would remember your sins no more. This is all thanks to Jesus and his finished work on the cross! As Jesus drew his last breath, he spoke and said, "It is Finished". Jesus was referring to the end of the law of sin and death (mistaken identity). Now, if God remembers your sins no more, and you are created in his very image, you then also forgive those who have sinned against you. I'm not saying it is always easy to forgive those who have hurt you. Forgiveness isn't only for the offender my friends; forgiveness is for you too! You see, if you hold onto anger and bitterness, it will only hinder your spiritual journey, you can not have love and unforgiveness in your heart simultaneously! Therefore, it is important that you forgive as soon as possible, even if you're not feeling it. Forgiveness does not mean that you tolerate abuse and you may even need to distance yourself in love from a person that is out to hurt you. I have heard it said that forgiveness is removing your hands from the offender's neck. You let go of the offense to Father. Not only is it important to forgive, but you should be aware that there is valid scientific evidence that unforgiveness causes the physical body to be under duress. This can cause elevated blood pressure, increased pulse, as well as many other physical ailments. Forgiving others releases the stress of carrying the burden in your physical body. Lastly, when you forgive you are freeing yourself spiritually, emotionally, and mentally as well. Do not beat yourself up if you are not able to forgive a situation all at one time. Forgiveness is often a process, and you will need help from the Spirit.

Memoir

Coming from an environment of trauma and abuse, I was hurt and broken in so many ways. Things that were said and things that were done to me haunted me for years of my life. I identified with shame which followed me through mid-adulthood. Once I was able to open my heart to trust again, Jesus was right there, prepared to heal me of the trauma I had suffered. During my healing, I realized I must forgive those who had caused me damage. Though my healing was already finished in the spiritual realm, this was not an overnight process. Jesus held my hand and my heart as I allowed myself to remember by opening my mind and heart to the Holy Spirit. It all came about as I became aware of God's love for me and his desire that I be whole. Since years of damage had been done, the process of healing took years. Near the end of this process, I let my abusers go to God. It is not my responsibility any longer. God's love everlasting has freed me to love and trust again.

Prayer

Father God, thank you for your forgiving nature. I am open to your Spirit to examine my heart and show me any unforgiveness that may be there hindering my spiritual journey or causing physical stress. I do not want to live in the bondage of unforgiveness any longer. Holy Spirit, lead me to let go of those who have caused me harm and give them to you. Teach me how to forgive so that I can be free on every level. Also, give me the wisdom to know when to move on from a relationship when it is not healthy. Help me to love at a distance when it is necessary. I will put all my trust in you. Jesus, you are the one that holds me together!

Song/YouTube: Forgiven: Crowder

Jesus At The Center

I have been crucified with Christ and I no longer live, but Christ lives in me. The life I now live in the body, I live by faith in the Son of God, who loved me and gave himself for me.
Galatians 2:20 (NIV)

When Jesus died, you died with him, burying all that was old, including the law that your forefathers lived by under the old covenant. When Jesus rose from the dead, you rose with him under the resurrection and a new covenant. You are a new creation; old things have passed away! Because of Jesus, the final sacrifice, the ten commandments and 613 sub laws became obsolete. Paul declares that you now live by faith in Jesus Christ, who loved you and gave his life for you. That my friends is the center of the gospel! Without Jesus, there would be no good news and the law of sin and death would still be in effect. You would still require animal sacrifices and the shedding of blood for forgiveness. However, you now live in freedom from the law and the regulations that accompanied it. It is because of Jesus that you have been restored and all things became new.

***

Memoir

    Surprisingly, I have come across many people who deny that Jesus is the center of the gospel or the center of their lives. I have heard people substitute words for Christ, such as source, vibrations, the universe, etc. Some say Jesus was only a historical figure in biblical times who was a teacher of biblical truths. Jesus has been removed from the middle of the gospel in these cases. Something that has been forgotten, is that Christ is 100% divine (God) and 100% human! So, it is with great hope that you have not given Jesus up as the very center of the gospel or as the center of your life! Simply speaking, Jesus is your everything, including the Truth, the Way, and the Life! Jesus is your path to our Father!

Prayer

    Father, help me to understand the purpose of Christ's life, death, and resurrection and how it relates to my life. Speak to my heart Jesus and speak the truth regarding your love for me. You loved me so much that you laid your life down so that I may live freely under the true gospel. My heart and mind are open to you to your resurrection power. Show me that the same Spirit Who raised Jesus from the dead lives within me!

Song/ YouTube: Jesus at the Center: David Funk

Chosen

But you are a chosen race, a royal priesthood, a holy nation, a people for his own possession, that you may proclaim the excellencies of him who called you out of darkness and into his marvelous light.
1 Peter 2:9 (ESV)

You have been hand chosen by God himself! He pursues you for his own, through the finished work of the cross. He called you from the darkness (thoughts of being separated from God) and you are now a child of the light. Praise him for the good things he has done in your life. You have been set aside by Abba as his possession and he has given himself to you freely. He is yours, and you are his!

Memoir
There was a long period of time in my life when I did not realize that I was chosen by God. I was very insecure, and I thought I had to do something to win Abba's approval and I had to work hard to be in his good graces. Basically, I thought I had to work for my salvation, God's approval,

and love. Oh, how wrong that type of thinking is! Today, I'm grateful that Father desires me as his possession.

Prayer

Jesus, give me a revelation of your love and approval over me. Show me that I am chosen by you! I am chosen and you desire me as your very own possession. I will proclaim your excellence oh God because you called me out of the darkness of my own thoughts of separation from you and brought me into the marvelous light!

Song/YouTube: Chosen Generation: Chris Tomlin

Restoration

In his kindness God called you to share in his eternal glory by means of Christ Jesus. So after you have suffered a little while, he will restore, support, and strengthen you, and will place you on a firm foundation.
1 Peter 5:10 (NLT)

So, you have used poor judgment, made a bad decision, and made mistakes? If so, you're probably beating yourself up and suffering from condemnation, guilt, and shame. But you will not suffer for long because Jesus is the restorer of all things in your life. In fact, one of the purposes of Jesus coming to earth was to restore all that had been lost! Even your mistakes will be restored by Jesus out of his great love for you. Even your human error can not thwart the restoration of Jesus over you. He restores all things by his generous love and grace and that love and grace is sufficient for you! He even cleans up the messes you have made in your humanness. Jesus has a reputation for turning all things in your favor! He makes ways where there seems to be no way. Nothing is impossible for God. Jesus is greater than your mistakes.

. . .

Memoir

There have been many times in my life when I have created my own messes! One example is when I made an incorrect career choice. I wanted to counsel people and felt God put that in my heart. It would take me over six years to complete my degree in counseling. I had already spent years working in a psychiatric unit, but I desired to spend more one-to-one time with my patients. I was a Behavioral Health Technician while attending college and I worked with several Registered Nurses at that time. Unbelievably, I allowed those nurses to talk me into going into nursing versus counseling. I chose to get my associate degree as a Registered Nurse in psychiatry. Eventually, the urge to be a Counselor resurfaced in me. Being a Therapist/Counselor had been placed in my heart by God. My heart sank as I realized my error in career choices. After working in the psychiatric unit for over twenty years as a nurse, I felt Abba wanted me to follow my heart's desire. With that in mind, I started courses at a Christian university. I first had to obtain my bachelor's degree in Family Life Education. I then moved forward to earn my master's degree in Counseling! All the while I maintained my job at the psychiatric hospital. My supervisors allowed me to start leading groups with my patients, which I enjoyed immensely. The university allowed me to earn clinical credits from the psychiatric hospital for my Counseling degree. Eventually, I began working as a Counselor for a local Christian counseling center. Even though I am now retired, I feel that I am exactly in the center of my heart's desire. All that education in college and the time I spent as a Psychiatric Nurse, prepared me for my life right now! God restored everything and I couldn't be any happier!

Prayer

Lord, you know I've made plenty of mistakes in my life. I trust that you have restored all things to my favor. Thank you that your mercies are new every morning! Jesus, I proclaim that you are my restorer! From this experience, I have learned to depend upon your voice in leading me, as you make a way, where there seems to be no way!

. . .

Song/YouTube: You Restore Everything: Rick Pino & Abbie Gamboa

God Is Approachable

Let us approach God's throne of grace with confidence, so that we may receive mercy and find grace to help us in time of need.
Hebrews 4:16 (NIV)

Many people have been taught that Abba is to be feared. The only fear we should feel in approaching our Father is that of immense awe of his Majesty. Others feel fear of God because they did not have a functional relationship with their earthly father. This skewed their view of God as the Father. However, something you can always count on is that Abba is the perfect Father! God always has your best in mind and his mercy and goodness are a continuous theme in your relationship with him. You can approach him with confidence because he desires to be with you! Oh, how he longs to have a relationship with you! His love for you is overwhelmingly powerful and it draws you to him. To approach Abba, all you have to do is look within yourself, for that is where his presence lives (we are God's temple). You are approved of by your Father; he greets you with great joy, mercy and acceptance. Your communion with him is what he most desires! Father created you so that he could love you and enjoy fellowship with you. Besides enjoying fellowship with him, we are told in scripture that we can boldly make our requests known to Abba. You have no reason to fear your loving Father!

Memoir

I did not have a relationship with my dad until the later years of his life. My dad was largely neglectful of me and never expressed love or kindness toward me. By observing him physically abuse my siblings, I learned very quickly in my younger years, to be a wallflower and avoid trouble at any cost. I literally feared my dad. I could not approach him about anything due to his temper and unpredictable behaviors. Unfortunately, this dysfunctional process led me to fear approaching God as my Father. I wasn't sure I could approach him and even thought of him as angry and disapproving of me. I also feared he would reject me due to the negligence I suffered from my dad.

The Holy Spirit showed me that Abba is approachable. As I came to understand his love and grace over me, I grasped that Father loved me and never tires of me spending time in his presence. My world became a place of light and life once my previous beliefs about God were eliminated. I experienced joy, freedom, love, grace, and peace all at one time! The dark veil that troubled me was lifted.

Today, I have a deep relationship with Abba. I no longer fear him as I know he's very approachable. I am his beloved and he is mine. Oh, how freeing it has been to become aware of the truth concerning the true nature of Abba!

Prayer

Oh, Father, I bring these precious ones before you. Demonstrate to them that you are a loving Papa who is approachable, kind, approving and accepting of me! Holy Spirit, move on the hearts of those who fear you *and think they cannot come to you openly and freely. Let them come into the understanding of your true nature. If any have been affected in their relationship with their earthly fathers, I pray for freedom from that bondage. Lord Jesus, I thank you that you set me free to have a sweet, open, and loving and deep relationship with you! Amen!*

Song/YouTube: Rest on Us: David Funk, Zahriya Zachary & Bryce Moore

Consider The Lilies

Observe how effortlessly wildflowers grow; they do not sweat or spin. Now, imagine the extravagant wardrobe of Solomon and his exquisite collection of brand-name clothes. I tell you; his most favorite robe would pale by comparison to any of these flowers.
Luke 12:27 (Mirror Bible)

In other words, God takes care of the beautiful lilies or wildflowers, so how much more will he take care of you? You have no need to worry about anything because Abba takes care of his children. He keeps his promises to you. Who are God's children? All are his children from before the foundation of the world! In this scripture, Jesus is saying not to be anxious over anything! God is Jehovah Jireh, meaning he will provide!

Memoir
I cannot list the many times abba has provided for me and my family in time of need. Even if we make mistakes, Abba is faithful to provide!

One very specific example is that I desperately needed to be free from my insecurities about relationships with my family and with God. I felt inadequate and unloved, Jehovah Jireh provided me with the truth and all my anxieties were resolved! If God is faithful to unravel a mess like this, then surely, he will provide whatever it is that you need in this life! As I grew in knowledge and wisdom of the true nature of my Father, I could clearly see all that he has provided in my past, even when I wasn't aware. I now realize God is my provider and I trust him to provide all I have needed for as long as I live on this earth. In reality and in the Spirit realm it's all already been done for us.

Prayer

Father, I'm open before you, and I will trust that you are Jehovah Jireh, my provider in my life. I will not depend upon myself to provide for my needs, but I will rely upon you, because you have always kept your promises, and your true nature is to love and keep me and care for me. You even care for the lilies of the fields and see each sparrow that falls. Oh! How much more you will care for me! I put my trust in you alone. Help me to see your goodness and love for me.

Song/ YouTube: Jireh: Chandler Moore & Naomi Raine

For The Brokenhearted

He heals the brokenhearted and binds up their wounds.
Psalms 147:3 (NKJV)

The LORD is close to the brokenhearted and saves those who are crushed in spirit.
Psalms 34:18 (NIV)

Are you crushed in spirit? Brokenhearted? Jesus came to restore you and your healing has already been taken care of, according to the finished work of the cross! You only need to become aware that he has healed your broken heart and bound up your wounds.

While Jesus was here on earth, He suffered in all the ways that you have suffered, and there is not one thing you have gone through, that Jesus is not familiar with. He knows your heart feels broken and that your spirit feels crushed. Furthermore, he understands and has provided your healing. Glory!

Memoir

Besides my own brokenness, I encountered many people who were broken and crushed in spirit through psychiatric nursing and in my role as a therapist. There is a popular saying, "hurting people, hurt people". This is so true! We have a tendency to project onto others, what we are experiencing ourselves. For example, when my husband and I first married, I was crushed in my spirit from the abuse and trauma I had endured, and I wasn't yet aware that Jesus had already taken care of this. I projected my feelings of brokenness onto my husband. Bless his heart! He is a patient and loving man. We accepted healing together, and we grew together. Jesus took away all my pain! My husband and I have been together since junior high school and have been married for 43 years now! It's all because of Jesus's healing power.in our marriage.

An old hymn comes to mind.

I must tell Jesus all my trials, I cannot bear these burdens alone. He kindly will help me, he ever loves and cares for his own, I must tell Jesus!"

Prayer

Father God, I will tell you all my troubles. I know you understand my brokenness and that my spirit has been crushed. I am aware that you are the only one who can help me. I experience your healing power for my pain. I intentionally let go of my suffering to you Jesus! I'm opening up to you in trust and confidence because I now realize that the same Spirit that raised Christ from the dead lives in me!

Song/YouTube: Broken People: Israel, New Breed & DOE

A Friend In Jesus

I do not communicate to you on a slave-boss basis; slaves have no clue what their masters are about to do. I talk to you as my friends, telling you everything I have heard in my conversion and intimate association with my Father. This I explain to you in the clearest possible terms.
John 15:15 (Mirror Bible)

Oh, what a friend we have in Jesus! We are in a perfect relationship with him. If you are having difficulty knowing Jesus is your friend, remember the disciple Judas, Even though Jesus knew Judas would betray him, he still called him a friend (Luke 22:48). This alone demonstrates the unconditional love and grace of Jesus for us! Jesus remains faithful to us even when we are unfaithful towards him (11 Timothy 2:13).

In the book of Proverbs, it states that Jesus is a friend that sticks closer than a brother. This is a true friend! He is closer to us than your own family, Jesus remains your friend even when we mess things up. That's the type of friend we need!

Memoir

Even though I had attended church from the age of four, I really didn't understand that Jesus was my friend. I learned this as an adult. To be honest, growing up in church, all I could hear was the condemnation and judgment that was spoken. So, my focus was on hell, sin, fear, demons, the devil, and the works I must do to earn my way to heaven without making any mistakes.

Very seldom was God's goodness spoken of and I didn't realize I had a friend in Jesus. When I came to Jesus with an open and wounded heart, he showed me that he was my friend. The compassion I experienced was incredible. I knew then that the love of Jesus for me was far greater than what I had previously learned, all the fear and condemnation fell away in my friendship with Jesus!

Prayer

Jesus, you have spoken the word that I am your friend. Thank you for being faithful to me, even in times when I was not faithful to you. I now know that true friendship isn't based on what I do, or what I do not do. In a true friendship, loyalty remains despite behavior. Your friendship with me is overwhelming and the warmth of this fills my heart! Father, reveal your friendship and love for me. Teach me that I love you because you first loved me.

Song/ YouTube: What A Friend We Have In Jesus: Aretha Franklin

Meditation Upon God

Finally, brothers, whatever is true, whatever is honorable, whatever is just, whatever is pure, whatever is lovely, whatever is excellent, if there be anything worthy of praise, think about these things.
Philippians 4:8 (ESV)

The very first mention of meditation upon God occurs in the book of Genesis and it means to muse, commune, and think deeply upon God. (Strong's Concordance)

Many think of meditation as a new-age term. This is simply not true! Meditation upon God has existed since the world was formed and man was created. Some find meditation difficult because they feel unable to focus their thoughts upon God. Mediation is a progressive act. The more you practice being still before God, the more the mind adapts. I encourage you to practice meditation upon Father because meditation brings forth revelation in the Spirit. Meditation is known to be the highest form of prayer. Meditation involves listening. If you listen, you will hear the voice of God speaking into your spirit.

Memoir

Previously I thought that meditation was a bad thing, I related it to the new-age movement. However, after researching the term, I found that meditation was in scripture over twenty times! I thought about Jesus going off by himself to be with Father. I don't think Jesus was doing most of the talking during these times. I believe Jesus was listening to Father's voice. Jesus said in scripture, that he only did and said what he had heard from his Father. Jesus must have done a whole lot of listening! When in meditation, I have found the answers to many questions, I have found guidance and direction, I have heard many revelations regarding the Trinity, I have found the solution to many of life's challenges in meditation. The most exciting thing of all that meditation upon God brings is the profound love that he pours out on me from within my union as one with him! I believe Meditation (listening) is one of the most important keys to intimacy with Jesus and my Father!

Prayer

Oh, Dear Father, teach me to listen to your voice in my life. Speak to me when I focus upon whatever is lovely in life and in the spiritual realm, whisper in my ear! Tell me great mysteries and tell me of your great love and grace for me. Bring me peace, guidance, direction, and fresh revelation from your heart to mine. Reveal the mysteries of the Spirit and give the keys to the Kingdom living!

Meditation/ YouTube: Christian Meditation for Sleep and Healing; find peace, calm & healing: Dan Musselman

Untitled

NOT MIGHT, NOR BY POWER, BUT BY MY SPIRIT

Then he told me, This is the word of the Lord to Zerubbabel: Not by might, nor by power, but by my Spirit, says the Lord of host.
Zechariah 4:6 (ESV)

Have you been attempting to do things by your own strength or power? Zerubbabel was! Until God spoke to him and told him he could not rely upon his own strength. Abba is saying the exact same thing to you today! Scripture points out that apart from God, you can do nothing. It's alright to rely totally on Abba for every situation in your life! The only thing you will accomplish in working to change your own circumstances is becoming frustrated. The sooner we realize that the power and strength come from Father, the sooner we see the manifestation of the answer to life problems.

So then, what's left for us to do? Absolutely nothing! We REST in the trust we have in Father to change ashes to beauty. You are embarking upon new territory, and you will see the goodness of God in the land of the living! It's not by your might, nor by your power, but by the Spirit of the Lord!

Memoir

I was extremely work-orientated in my past. I worked myself to the bone in church activities and in my personal life in order to change the outcome of my situations. I wanted to please God, justify myself, to make myself worthy in Abba's eyes., I thought I had to earn my way to heaven. Jesus showed me that quite the opposite is true, My responsibility is to rest in trusting Jesus's finished work on the cross. My responsibility is to let go of all that concerns me to Father. Remember to consider the lilies!

Prayer

Lord, teach me to avoid all self-effort in order to please you and gain approval from you. Help me to realize that I can put my trust in you. Let your approval of me be clear! You take care of me. out of your great love for me! I already have your approval & your full acceptance exactly where I am now. Let me remember that it is not my own power or might that the situations in my life change. It is only through your Spirit!

Song/YouTube: Your Spirit: Tasha Cobbs Leonard & Kierra Sheard

Praise And Worship

Give thanks to the Lord, for he is good; his love endures forever. Who can proclaim the mighty acts of the LORD or fully declare his praise?
Psalms 106:1 (NIV)

Many people who have turned from organized religion, are now turned off by worship and praise. They tell me it reminds them of the church with all the rules, regulations, and hypocrisy,

We have to be cautious that we don't throw out everything we ever learned about God away in the deconstructed process when leaving organized religion. Multiple people want to toss out praise and worship of God because of their bad experiences in the church, but there are specific things we should hold onto, and praise and worship are definitely at the top of the list. We simply can't throw out the baby with the bathwater!

. . .

Praise and worship of Jesus are not only for him, but he makes it about us too. Something mysterious takes place during praise and worship! The glory of God seems to shine more brightly, and peace floods our souls. You see, as we are worshiping God, he's telling us that he adores us and loves us too. Praise and worship elevate us to the realm of the Spirit. Gratitude and anxiety, or depression are incapable of existing in our minds simultaneously. As we worship, we lift Jesus up and show our gratitude, he lifts us up too. I have witnessed people set free their issues during praise and worship.

Memoir

I have discovered that praise and worship unto God may not change my circumstance, but it changes my perspective regarding my situation! As I worship, peace, joy, and comfort fill my being with light, love, and reassurance of God's presence within me. Scripture points out that if we don't praise him, the rocks will cry out and the trees will clap their hands! I'm going to continue with praise and worship. It changes my perspective, and I can more easily put on the mind of Christ regarding my circumstances. Lift Jesus up and watch how communing with him in praise and worship changes your perspective of life! It's not God who changes during praise and worship, it's me who is changed!

Prayer

Father God, teach me that praising and worshiping you is not something I simply throw away as a bad memory from the past. I will freely worship you in spirit and in truth! Manifest yourself to me in all your power and glory. I lift you high Lord, high above my mind and high above my heart. Oh God, as I magnify you, manifest your peace, love, and joy in my spirit. I will exalt you and my perspective will be having the mind of Christ!

Song/ YouTube: I'm Gonna Worship: Dante Bowe & Maryanne J. George

Self-Effort

So, then it depends not on human will or exertion, but on God, who has mercy.
Romans 9:16 (ESV)

It's very seldom that self-effort pays off. Striving to obtain it is futile! God does not depend upon our will to bless us or in giving us his kingdom. Effort and striving are what we do when we do not understand the concept of God's blessings and grace. He has already given us everything that pertains to life & happiness through the finished work of the cross! We simply need to come to a point when we rest in knowing that God's kingdom is ours and that he's already provided for all we have need of. There's no need to strife or work beyond this. His grace is sufficient for us all!

In reality, our striving gets in the way of hearing God's Voice because we're too busy to listen.

. . .

Memoir

Oh my, did I ever used to strive! I worked hard in church activities, and in my personal life. I prayed hard in my prayer closet, I called out to get through my emotions, I didn't leave my prayer time until I had an emotional breakthrough. That meant lots of striving, begging, pleading and so forth. I didn't realize Christ lived directly within me, and I could have spoken to him at any given moment. I behaved that way because II thought God was distant from me. I stopped working and striving when I became aware that Jesus was living within me, and I was his dwelling place. I still talk to God and Jesus frequently, but now it is so much different. We are on a continuous journey of love and communion with one another. No striving to enter into his presence!

Prayer

Father, teach me that you are not a distant God, but that you live within me. I am your temple, and I can fellowship with you at any time . Help me to see the areas where I'm striving and show me how to let go of that self-effort, by becoming aware that you are omnipresent. I don't have the responsibility to fix my own issues, because you are always working on my behalf to turn all things for my good. I will lean upon you Jesus because you have restored all things! Teach me that it is not by my human will, but on the will of my Father who has mercy.

Song/ YouTube: God Will Work It Out: Maverick City Music, Lyric video

God Is Good

The Lord is good to all; he has compassion for all he has made.
Psalms 145 (NIV)

As we previously discussed, God's nature is love and therefore good! He is rich in mercies that endure forever. The character of God is unchanging and there is no shadow of turning. God is love and he cannot go against his nature, or he would be denying himself, which is love. Abba's goodness is over ALL he created, including you, my friend! His goodness follows hard in pursuit of you.

Memoir

I once thought that God was particular in who he blessed and was good over, and this did not include me. I was double minded about God's goodness and kindness because I thought he was good to others but condemned me.

. . .

Then the Holy Spirit led me to realize that the word ALL meant ALL and did include me! Oh, what a joyous occasion that was! I will never forget when I found that God Loved me and was good to me out of his nature.

Prayer

Oh, sweet Holy Spirit, manifest your goodness in my life and give me eyes to see your true nature is forever loving. Thank you for showing your goodness over ALL, including me! Help me to see your goodness and give me the ability to pass your goodness on to others who are struggling with the concept of your kindness in their lives.

Song/YouTube: Goodness of God: Jenn Johnson, Live

Grace To All

DEDICATED TO MY FRIEND PAUL GRAY

For out of his fullness (abundance) we have ALL received (all had a share and we were all supplied with) one grace after another and spiritual blessing upon spiritual blessing and even
John 1:16 (AMPC)

Grace is defined as showing favor for *all*. God is favorably inclined towards you! Abba is always gracious to all. In the Hebrew language, the word grace is defined as chanan, which means *a state of kindness*, and the Greek word is charis, defined as *favor*. This means that God's grace, favor and kindness are over you all the time. These attributes of God come from his abundance and are given to us in one grace after another, and one blessing after another.

Memoir

I understand that many people feel God is vengeful against his children. I used to believe that the same way! I changed my mind (repented) about this thought process. God is not double-minded or bipolar! He cannot be loving and gracious and then torment his children forever without mercy. He's either loving or not, he's either gracious or not, but it can't be two ways, For God is love and God never changes his mind about us! Besides all of this, there is nothing we can do to earn these things, grace and love are a gift from our Father. Abba doesn't take back the gifts he has imparted unto us.

Prayer

Thank you, Father, for your loving kindness over me, and thank you for your graciousness over me. Your mercies are new every single morning and great is your faithfulness. Your grace and love are overwhelming, and I rejoice that I'm included in your favor and blessing which flows freely unto me!

Song/YouTube: ByThe Grace Of God: Brian and Jenn Johnson, Lyric Video

The Vine & The Branches

I Am the vine, and you are the branches; It is the one who understands this mutual union that naturally bears more fruit -which is impossible to happen apart from me.
John 15:5 (Mirror Bible)

Independently of Christ, we can do nothing, But all the branches (us) in the vine (Jesus) produce fruit. We produce fruit in our union together, as one! We were not created outside of the vine, but IN the vine (Christ). The vine provides the branches with the care they need to produce much good fruit! The branches are unable to produce fruit without the vine. To further illustrate this point, a good pastor friend of mine said it this way, " God is the ocean, and we are the waves (Don Keathley). The waves (us) could not exist without the ocean (God).

Memoir
I have known people to take this verse out of context. Some underrate their position as the branches. These people are unable to understand that

they are connected to Abba as the vine. They do not comprehend that they are in union with God and that good fruit is produced within this union. Please understand that the vine and branches are vital to one another, and that we are in co-union with Christ. Therefore, we function to produce an abundance of good fruit together!

On the other end of the spectrum, are those who believe that they are I AM (God), due to our oneness in him (co-union). However, we are only one in him as the branches connected to the vine! We work together in union. Our Father will always be the head (the vine), which is essential to the branches (us). One cannot be the vine, because there is only ONE vine, who is God. We were created in his image, not as his duplicate. Our identity is in him, but we are not Abba.

As a believer, I identified with our first analogy, I did not grasp the fact that I was in Christ as the branch. I had no self-worth, and I had no clue of my standing in Christ. After my healing manifested, I finally took up my position as the branch in the vine!

Prayer

Lord, help me to understand my seamless union in you. You created me as your branch, and you have always been the vine! Let all confusion about this be placed far from me. I know we will bear good fruit together! For in you, I live, move, and have my being!

Song/YouTube: Abide In Me: Andrew Marcus, Lyric Video

Resurrection Life

Our union with Christ further reveals that because the same spirit that awakened the body of Jesus from the dead inhabits us, we equally participate in his resurrection. In the same act of authority whereby God raised Jesus from the dead, co-restores your body to life by his indwelling spirit.
Romans 8:11 (Mirror Bible)

Oh, how very exciting! The same spirit that raised Christ from the dead, dwells in you! To recognize this, is to be aware that you have resurrection life within you as God's temple! I don't know how much better this can get! There is nothing for you to do to gain this resurrection life, because it existed in you from before time began when you were already in God's creative plan.

This Spirit is powerful and functions from the love of God for his children. Just as Abba raised Christ from the dead, he raised you from the dead too. Remember, when Jesus died, our old nature died with him, and as he rose from the dead, you rose with him as a new creation. That's the resurrection power in you!

Memoir

As I became a whole (healed) person in Christ, these scriptures became alive for me! Once I learned that the same power that raised Jesus from the dead, dwelled in me, and hasn't changed for over two-thousand and years, I was more than elated. I then began to see difficult situations in my life change, because my perception changed, and I know I have resurrection power within me!

Prayer

Abba (Daddy), thank you for my co-resurrection in Christ. Make me aware of the power that dwells in me! I will not strive to obtain this power, because it is already within me. When Jesus rose from the dead, I arose a new creation. This Spirit quickens my mortal body, brings wisdom and knowledge, comfort, wholeness and pertains to every level of my life! I have resurrection power living inside of me!

Song/ YouTube: Resurrecting Live: Elevation Music

The God Who Never Changes

Of old you laid the foundations of the earth, and the heavens are the work of your hands. They will perish, but you will remain; they will wear out like a garment. You will change them like a robe, and they will pass away, but you are the same and your years have no end.
Psalms 102:25-27 (KJV)

Father is the same, yesterday, today, and forever (Hebrews 13:8). Situations in your life will change, circumstances may change, and you will change from glory to glory in Christ. Thank God that he never has changed, and he never will! This is something you can grab ahold of something you can be assured of! The fact that Abba never changes will make you secure in your salvation and in every area of your life. He is reliable, dependable, and trustworthy. He always has been and always will be!

Memoir
From childhood to mid-adulthood, my life changed from moment to

moment. It was totally unpredictable, There was nothing I could hold onto due to my lack of knowledge, and I never felt secure. In fact, I never knew what to expect next. This caused me to experience confusion and doubt. I dreaded going to sleep at night because I didn't know what the next day would hold. I dreaded waking up in the mornings, because I never knew what might happen on that day. I was sure of nothing.

Once I understood the fact that Father never changes, I was assured of my security in Christ! God was someone I could depend on to be the same from day to day. I knew what I could expect from Abba, and it was always good! What I would expect was to be loved, day in and day out! I then went to bed at night in expectation of joy in the morning. I woke up excited to be with Jesus each day. I lived my life to the absolute fullest! No more dread, anxiety, or fear of what may happen next. My life was in the hands of my Father, and I knew he remained the same!

Prayer

Father, demonstrate your stability in my life. I know you are always the same! I will be secure in your love! I can feel secure in you because you never change your mind about me. Everything remains the same...goodness all the way around! Assure me that you are indeed reliable, dependable, and my security is in you! Thank you for your trustworthiness! Thank you for never changing how you feel about me!

Discussion/YouTube: God Never Changes: Josh Weidmann

Guilt Versus Shame

So, now there is no condemnation for those who belong to Christ Jesus.
Romans 8:1 (NLT)

There is a vast difference between guilt and shame. Guilt comes when we've done something wrong. The answer to resolving guilt, is to repent (have a change of mind). You need to ask for forgiveness from the person you offended. You then need to move on from guilt, whether this person accepts your request for forgiveness or not. The point is that you do not carry guilt in your heart.

Shame is a different thing altogether. Shame states, "there is something wrong with me". Unfortunately, many use shame as a weapon to control others. It is used to keep people in a state of low self-esteem. As long as you feel shameful, your thoughts are consumed by this ugly beast. If you feel unworthy, it will definitely hinder the truth of the gospel from coming alive in you. This is an identity crisis! The key to ridding yourself of shame is to realize WHO YOU ARE IN CHRIST! You are a son/daughter of God! You are awesome in Abba's eyes, and he adores you just as you are. Shame is powerful, but not more powerful than the truth of who you are in Christ. Overcome shame by learning who you are, and who you belong to!

Memoir

Experiencing shame was one of my biggest struggles. I was shamed as a child by my parents and condemned by religion. When I was a small child, I used to stay behind my mother's skirts to hide myself from people. When I was in junior high school, I literally walked down the halls with my hand over my face. You see, my shame was so powerful that I thought people could see what I was ashamed about, so I tried to hide myself.

What was all that shame about? I couldn't quite put my finger on anything I had done wrong. I haven't hurt anyone, and I didn't have anything to repent of.

The shame was a problem of not understanding my true identity in Christ. Shame can blind a person to the truth.

Later in life, I learned who I truly was. I am a daughter of God, and his righteousness is in me, because of what he did for me. I am holy, redeemed, restored, and without shame! There is therefore NOW no condemnation to those who are in Christ Jesus.

Prayer

Jesus, thank you for showing me who I truly am in Christ, the savior of the world. I'm grateful that you have delivered me from the damage of shame! You are the one who makes me whole from any shame I have experienced in my life. Show me through your Spirit that I am restored because you restore all that was lost. Lord, my self-worth was lost, but you have come to my rescue! I will not accept shame in my life any longer! Shame is not of you God, rather shame comes from man. I put my trust in Jesus, and trust that I've been delivered from shame once and for all! Amen!

Song/YouTube: I Am Your Beloved: Jonathan David & Melissa Helser

Deep Calls To Deep

Deep calls to deep at the sound of your waterfalls; all your breakers and your waves have rolled over me.
Psalms 42:7 (NASB)

Deep calling to Deep represents God's Spirit calling to the deepest part of your spirit. Waterfalls are thunderous, and the waves and breakers represent obstacles you may face. The Psalmist is stating that even though he faced many blockades, God protected him through it all.

When God calls to you, through his Spirit, he's communicating to your spirit and coaxing you through to victory, despite what may stand in your way.

Another view of this scripture is that when things are changing, it may not feel comfortable for you. The Psalmist was exiting from the predicament he was in, but he faced many obstacles. That had to be uncomfortable. However, he said he was protected from all that came against him. The process of change is not always pleasant, even when that change is for the better. There will be obstacles, but Abba will see you through safety.

When God calls to you deeply from his Spirit, your spirit will be moved! You will know without doubt that Abba is urging you forward in your spiritual growth!

Memoir
God's Spirit called deeply to my spirit when he asked me to leave religion behind and follow him. I was in a very uncomfortable position. My brother was my pastor and I loved him deeply. I had attended his church for over fifteen years. It was a lifelong dream to be under my brother's ministry. It felt uncomfortable to tell him I was leaving, and I was not without fear. There were obstacles. My brother was hurt, I was hurt, and things were awkward between us for years after that.

Hallelujah! God brought both of us through that situation. God restored our relationship, and we are now closer than we were before! There were also many obstacles during my change from religion to grace. God desired to heal me of my past abuse. During the healing process, I had to face many demons from my past. But Abba brought me through them all! The waterfalls were thunderous, and the waves and breakers were intimidating, but God caused them to roll over me, and I was unharmed in the safety of his love and grace!

Prayer
Abba, help me to be willing to grow. Help me to listen to deep calling deep! Though change in my life may be uncomfortable, and I may face obstacles, I know that you will cause those obstacles to roll away over me and I will be victorious!

. . .

Song/YouTube: Deep Cries Out: William Matthews, Bethel Music

No Separation

This is my conviction; no threat whether it be in death or life; be it celestial messengers, demon powers, or political principalities, nothing known to us at this time, or even unknown in the future. ^{39} no dimension of any calculation in time or space, nor any device yet to be invented, has what it takes to separate us from the love of God demonstrated in Christ. The Lordship of Jesus Christ is our ultimate authority.
Romans 8:38-39 (Mirror Bible)

Abba Father has a deep agape love for you! He adores you just as you are right now, despite what you may think of yourself. Nothing has the power to separate you from his love. Nothing can stop his love from pursuing your heart. Very simply, God will never cease from loving you, even if you do not love him in return. But listen to this. Scripture points out that you love him because he first loved you. I believe with the power of the Holy Spirit; you will participate in God's undying love for you. That's what agape love is all about. A loving relationship between you and Abba!

. . .

Memoir

Though I attended church for most of my life, I had difficulty grasping that Abba loved me. All I could see were conditions between us. I would think, "God loves, but he is just...God loves me if I do this...God loves me and... he sends those he those he loves to hell if they make a mistake. The list went on and on!

The truth was God's love for me began before the foundations of this world. He created me from love! Once I let go of the conditions, God's love was so incredibly apparent to me. He literally poured his loving heart over me in demonstration of his love for me!

Prayer

Father, manifest your great love for me! I'm asking in expectation of your answer. Show me that your love is without conditions and that nothing in heaven or earth can separate me from your love! Flood my spirit with your love and we will walk together in an agape relationship forever!

Song/YouTube: I Can't Get Away & Downpour: Melissa Helser & Naomi Raine

A Way For Me

I Am the LORD who opens a way through the waters, making a dry path through the sea.
Isaiah 43:16 (NLT)

No matter what circumstances you are in, even if you created your own issues, God is present to make a way out for you! He makes ways where there seems to be no way. That's experiencing the love and grace of a kind Father! Mercy follows after us and mercy is new every morning. This is an amazing & miraculous trait of your Father. When you're in the midst of a problem, God will not tell you, "You made your bed, now lay in it". No, that's not the way of your Father! God restored all that was lost through Jesus. If you've lost your way, depend upon God to get you out, even if you see no way out!

Memoir

In my former years, I worried consistently if the way out of a situation seemed hopeless. But I did find a way of escaping from every blockage in my path. It was through Jesus! I found that no matter what difficulty I was facing, it always turned out the very best for me. That was me becoming aware that God was always making way for me. My worry was fruitless! God's goodness and mercy was consistently making ways for me. I closely observed my paths through life and discovered that I had not once sank in the waters!

Prayer

Dearest Abba, help me to open my eyes to your generous nature. Show me your loving kindness in always making my paths straight, even if I mess up! I know now that you are the restorer of all things in my life. Let me observe that your mercies are new every morning and you are always making ways for me where I am unable to see a way!

Song/YouTube: Way Maker: Paul McClure

A Living Hope

Praise be to God and Father of our Lord Jesus! In his great mercy he has given us a new birth in a Living Hope through the resurrection of Jesus from the dead.
1 Peter 1:3 (NIV)

Let's think about this for a moment. Of all the gods who were worshiped throughout the ages, Jesus is the only one who had resurrection power within him. This resurrection power is derived from Abba alone! Jesus rose from the dead on your behalf! This is where your salvation lies. This is the genuine New Birth You are not saved by saying a magical prayer that allows you into God's good graces. You were chosen in Christ before the foundations of the cosmos. You have always been in Christ Jesus, but you were told that you were saved by saying the sinner's prayer. My friends, salvation does not depend upon what you do, rather salvation depends on what Jesus has already done! Jesus is alive and sitting on God's right side because his work is finished. You have risen with Jesus in a *new birth*!! This is your LIVING HOPE!

. . .

Memoir

In the past, I genuinely believed that everyone had to repeat the sinner's prayer to be saved. Because of this belief, I reached out to many who were sick or dying to make sure that they said the sinner's prayer in order to make it to heaven. When I look back on this, I can see that I was operating out of fear of never seeing my loved ones again after they passed from this life. You see, with this particular theology, I viewed some people in, and some people out of God's kingdom. It's an "us and them" theology. I wanted everybody in God's kingdom. So, I went about making sure everyone said the sinner's prayer. The Holy Spirit corrected me on this way of thinking. Yes, every knee shall bow, and every tongue will confess that Jesus is Lord, but that is not how we become saved. We were saved in the resurrection of Jesus, the SAVIOR of the WORLD! We have a Living Hope in Jesus, due to his life, death, and resurrection to life again! Jesus is still alive today and you are included in the kingdom of God!

Prayer

Oh Jesus! Thank you for being my Living Hope. Thank you for your life, death and resurrection on my behalf. Because you live today, I live also. I was given a new birth in the resurrection! Abba, show me that my salvation is not based on anything I can do, rather, my salvation is founded on what you've already done for me.

Song/YouTube: Living Hope: David Funk, Moment

Conclusion

Now that you have read through these pages, my hope is that you have seen the *true nature* of God. God's true character is good and his love and grace for you are limitless! May you see Jesus as your *Living Hope* and that your life is in the resurrection of him who came to restore you. I pray that you are delivered from fear, shame, guilt, and condemnation. Be easy on yourself! Don't be discouraged if you need to go back through the devotional because there is a lot of new information here to digest, especially since you may have been in bondage with your previous environment and religious teachings.

Of all the hopes I have for you, my *greatest* is that you see yourself as whole through the finished work of the cross in Christ! Jesus is the way, truth, and life! He is the mediator between you and Abba. Jesus is the center of your life!

God is continuously changing ashes to beauty! Speak his healing power into your life over the trauma and abuse you endured, Speak love, grace, peace, and beauty over yourself as affirmations are highly encouraged and effective. The power of restoration to health and well-being is reinforced as you speak God's word into your being.

As you allow the Holy Spirit to work on your behalf, you will begin to see a change of heart and mind within yourself. That's the resurrection power of Jesus restoring you to your original design in God. The best advice I can give you as you read through this devotional is to *let go* of everything you previously thought you knew about God and yourself! You are now walking in new horizons and the beauty of the wholeness of the Spirit.

Coming Soon!

From Ashes to Beauty:
Recovering From Trauma and Abuse Through The Spirit **Workbook!**

www.thewriterssociety.online

The Writer's Society is an assisted self publishing company empowering authors to release books that reveal God's goodness to the world through a variety of self publishing services.

Made in United States
Orlando, FL
27 November 2022